I0017284

MacBook Air 2025 (M4) User Guide

The Step-By-Step Manual For Beginners & Seniors To Set Up, Navigate, And Master The Apple Mac With M4-Chip. With Essential MacOS Sequoia Tips & Tricks

Matt E. Walker

Copyright © 2025 Matt E. Walker

All rights reserved. This book should not be reproduced, shared, or distributed in any format—whether electronic, print, or mechanical—without express permission from the writer or publisher. Limited exceptions apply for brief excerpts used in reviews, analysis, or other legally permitted, non-commercial uses.

Any unauthorized reproduction, distribution, or use of this content is strictly forbidden and may lead to legal consequences, including potential claims for damages by the writer or publisher.

This book is an independent publication and has no affiliation with, endorsed by, or connected to Apple Inc. It is intended solely for informational and unofficial purposes.

Table of Contents

INTRODUCTION

Apple's latest refresh of its fan-favorite MacBook Air just raised the bar—again. With a powerful new M4 chip under the hood, a dramatically improved webcam, and a welcome drop in price, the 2025 MacBook Air makes an even stronger case for being the best all-around laptop you can buy.

Starting at £999 / $999 / €1,199, the new 13-inch model is £100 cheaper than its predecessor—yet it comes loaded with significant upgrades. Right out of the box, you get Apple's next-gen M4 processor and 16GB of memory as the new base standard, meaning the entry-level model is no longer a compromise.

Design & Display: Familiar Looks, Fresh Color

Externally, the design has remained unchanged since 2022, keeping that impossibly slim and light aluminum body. The real news is the stylish new light blue finish, which replaces the long-standing "space grey" option. It still houses the best-in-class trackpad, ultra-responsive keyboard, and fast Touch ID sensor.

The 13.6-inch LCD is bright, crisp, and sharp—but still capped at 60Hz. While that's perfectly fine for most users, competitors with high-refresh-rate screens may appeal more to gamers or those craving super-smooth visuals.

Camera & Performance

This year, Apple gave the webcam some serious love. The new 12MP Centre Stage camera is perfect for video calls, using smart tech to automatically frame and follow your face. It even supports Desk View, letting you share what's on your desk like a mini overhead cam—great for demos or online teaching.

Underneath it all, the M4 chip delivers blazing-fast performance that nearly matches the MacBook Pro. Even without fans, the Air stays cool and silent during heavy tasks. While the entry model has two fewer GPU cores, it's still plenty powerful for everything short of high-end workstation tasks or advanced gaming.

Apple also bumped the base RAM to 16GB, which is finally in line with what modern multitasking demands. Last year, you had to pay £200 just to go from 8GB to 16GB—now it's standard.

Battery Life

Battery life remains a standout feature. For typical tasks like web browsing, documents, chatting, and media, the Air routinely delivers 16+ hours of use on a single charge. Push it harder—think photo editing or light coding—and it still holds strong for 10+ hours. Two full workdays, unplugged.

Specs at a Glance

Display: 13.6" LCD (2560x1600, 224 PPI), True Tone

1) Processor: Apple M4 (8-core or 10-core GPU)
2) Memory: 16GB, 24GB, or 32GB
3) Storage: 256GB to 2TB SSD
4) OS: macOS Sequoia 15.4
5) Camera: 12MP with Centre Stage
6) Ports: 2x Thunderbolt/USB 4, headphone jack, MagSafe
7) Connectivity: Wi-Fi 6E, Bluetooth 5.3
8) Weight: 1.24kg
9) Dimensions: 304.1 x 215 x 11.3mm

Sustainability & Repairability

Apple is also making strides on the eco front. The M4 MacBook Air is made from 55% recycled materials, including metals like aluminum and copper, along with rare earth elements. The battery is replaceable (£159), and iFixit rates it a 5/10 for repairability—average, but better than some rivals. Apple's trade-in and recycling programs still apply, even for non-Apple products.

Smarter Than Ever

Running macOS Sequoia 15.4, the Air benefits from Apple's newest features like AI-powered email sorting, smarter notification summaries, and iPhone mirroring. The redesigned Mail app brings a more iPhone-like feel, while new window snapping and tiling tools make multitasking easier without third-party apps.

Pricing and Value

1) 13" MacBook Air M4: from £999 / $999 / €1,199
2) 15" version: from £1,199 / $1,199 / €1,499
3) For context, the M4 MacBook Pro starts at £1,599, the Samsung Galaxy Book 4 Edge costs £1,399, and Microsoft's new Surface Laptop 7 starts at £1,049. So the Air remains competitive—even aggressively priced—for a premium machine.

A New Gold Standard

The 2025 MacBook Air is a no-brainer for anyone not tied to Windows. It hits that sweet spot of performance, battery life, build quality, and now value, like no other. The M4 chip puts it nearly on par with the Pro while keeping everything featherlight and whisper-quiet. Add in the upgraded webcam and extra memory, and this Air is not just refined—it's future-ready.

Sure, it's not perfect—only two USB-C ports, no SD card slot or Face ID—but for most users, those are minor trade-offs. For the price, you're getting a laptop that feels like it should cost hundreds more.

Pros: Lightning-fast M4 chip, excellent battery, sleek and silent design, fantastic webcam, top-notch keyboard and trackpad, upgraded memory, beautiful display.

Cons: Just two USB-C ports, no USB-A or SD slot, no Face ID, non-upgradable RAM/SSD, no Wi-Fi 7.

CHAPTER ONE

HOW TO USE THE MAC CONTROL CENTER IN MACOS

With macOS Big Sur, Apple gave the Mac interface a fresh new feel—one of the standout features being the redesigned Control Center. Borrowing inspiration from iOS, it offers a sleek, centralized hub for quick access to your most-used settings, all just a click away.

How to Find It

Look to the top-right corner of your screen and you'll spot the Control Center icon in the menu bar. Click it, and up pops a panel full of handy controls like Wi-Fi, Bluetooth, AirDrop, Do Not Disturb, Keyboard Brightness, and Screen Mirroring. Each icon acts as a shortcut—click one, and you'll see its full settings right there. For example, tap on Wi-Fi to view and connect to available networks on the fly.

You'll also find sliders for Volume and Display Brightness, making it easy to fine-tune your setup. Plus, if you're playing music, there's a built-in media control section to pause, skip, or play your favorite tracks directly from the Control Center.

How to Customize It Your Way

One of the coolest tricks? You can drag your favorite controls from the Control Center directly onto the menu bar for even faster access. Just click and drag. Want to remove one? Hold down the Command key, and then drag it off the bar—easy!

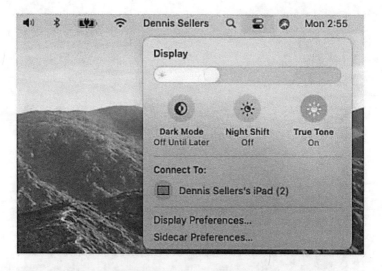

Fine-Tuning the Experience

While customization in Big Sur is somewhat limited, Apple does give you a few options. To tweak your Control Center:

1) Click the Apple menu in the top-left corner of your screen.
2) Choose System Preferences > Dock & Menu Bar.
3) Here, you'll see two key sections:
   a) Control Center: These items are always shown in the Control Center, though you can choose whether they also appear in the menu bar.
   b) Other Modules: These are optional extras—like Battery or Accessibility Shortcuts—that you can add by checking "Show in Control Center" or "Show in Menu Bar."

c) With just a few clicks, you can tailor your Control Center to match your workflow—so the settings you need are always within easy reach.

M3 VS M4 MACBOOK AIR: WHICH ONE TO BUY?

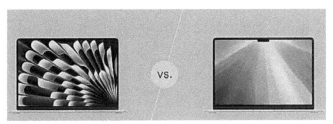

Thinking about upgrading your laptop? Apple's M3 and M4 MacBook Air models both pack a serious punch—but each is built with a different kind of user in mind. Whether you're diving into creative projects or just need a reliable machine for daily tasks, here's a side-by-side comparison to help you choose the best fit.

What Sets Them Apart?

a) M4 MacBook Air
b) Blazing-fast 10-core CPU
c) Up to 32 GB of memory
d) Dual external display support
e) Upgraded 12MP camera with Desk View

f) Exclusive Sky Blue color option

M3 MacBook Air

a) Solid 8-core CPU
b) Up to 24 GB of memory
c) Supports one external display
d) Standard high-def camera

Available in Space Gray and other classic colors

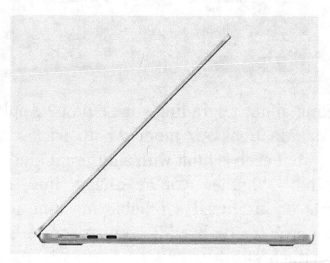

The M4 MacBook Air is aimed at those who need a little more power and polish, while the M3 model keeps things simple, sleek, and efficient.

Performance Showdown: Power Users vs. Everyday Warriors

The M4 steps up with a 10-core CPU and 10-core GPU, giving it the kind of processing muscle that's perfect for editing 4K videos, managing massive spreadsheets, or running pro apps side by side. It also supports up to 32 GB of RAM, which makes multitasking smooth even under pressure.

The M3, though, isn't far behind for general use. It features an 8-core CPU and can handle 24 GB of RAM, which is more than enough for everyday productivity, streaming, casual content creation, and more. But if you're pushing your system to the max, the M4 has the edge.

Display & Camera: Visual Upgrades That Matter

1) M4 MacBook Air

a) Crisp 12MP webcam with Center Stage and Desk View (great for pros on calls)
b) Supports two high-res external displays (finally!)
c) Available in the eye-catching Sky Blue

2) **M3 MacBook Air**
a) Standard 1080p webcam
b) Supports one external display (unless you close the lid)
c) Comes in classic colors, including Space Gray

If you're frequently on Zoom or like to work across multiple monitors, the M4's upgrades are hard to ignore. The Desk View feature even lets you share what's on your desk during calls—ideal for demos or teaching.

Connectivity, Storage & Other Specs: Mostly a Draw

Both laptops offer:

a) Wi-Fi 6E and Bluetooth 5.3
b) Two Thunderbolt 4 (USB-C) ports
c) Up to 2 TB of SSD storage

The main difference here is memory. The M4 offers more RAM (32 GB max), which makes it more future-proof for heavy multitaskers and creatives.

Which One Should You Get?

Go with the M4 MacBook Air if:

1) You work with resource-heavy apps or multitask constantly
2) You need dual-display support or a better webcam
3) You want the latest and greatest Apple has to offer

Stick with the M3 MacBook Air if:

1) You're looking for excellent performance at a lower price
2) You mainly browse, stream, create light content, and take occasional video calls
3) You don't need multiple external displays

At the end of the day, both are fantastic machines. If budget isn't a concern and you want peak performance with modern features, the M4 MacBook Air is a no-brainer. But if you're happy with a lighter workload and want to save a bit without sacrificing too much, the M3 MacBook Air is still a rock-solid choice.

HOW TO TURN ON AIRDROP MAC

AirDrop is one of Apple's handiest features — it lets you share photos, videos, documents, websites, and more between your Apple devices in just a few taps or clicks. Whether you're sending something from your iPhone to a friend's iPad, or from your Mac to your iPhone, AirDrop makes the process super smooth.

But before you can start flinging files across the air, you'll need to make sure AirDrop is turned on. Here's how to do it — step-by-step.

How to Turn On AirDrop

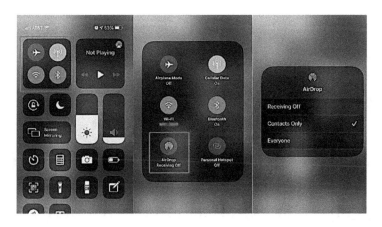

Before diving into the settings, make sure Wi-Fi and Bluetooth are enabled on both the device you're sending from and the one receiving. Also, make sure Personal Hotspot is turned off — it can interfere with AirDrop.

Quick Steps:

1) Open the Control Center
2) On iPhone X or later, and iPad with Face ID: Swipe down from the upper-right corner of the screen.
3) On older iPhones or iPads: Swipe up from the bottom.
4) Press and hold the section with the Airplane Mode, Wi-Fi, and Bluetooth icons — this will expand the panel.
5) Tap on AirDrop.
6) Choose either:

a) Contacts Only (more private)
b) Everyone (easier if you're not in each other's contacts)
c) Once selected, the AirDrop icon should turn blue, meaning it's good to go!

If you choose Contacts Only, both devices need to be signed into iCloud, and your contact info (like email or phone number) needs to be saved on the other person's device.

How to Enable AirDrop on a Mac

AirDrop works great on macOS too whether you're transferring files to another Mac or an iPhone. First things first: make sure Wi-Fi and Bluetooth are switched on.

To check:

1) Look at the top-right menu bar and click on the Wi-Fi or Bluetooth icon to turn it on.
2) Or, go to System Preferences > Network or Bluetooth if you don't see the icons.

Once that's sorted, here's how to turn on AirDrop:

1) If you're using macOS Big Sur or later:
2) Click the Control Center icon (top right of your screen).
3) Click AirDrop.
4) Toggle it ON.
5) Choose who can see your device:
6) Contacts Only
7) Everyone

On older macOS versions:

1) Open a Finder window.
2) In the left-hand sidebar, click AirDrop.
3) At the bottom of the window, you'll see "Allow me to be discovered by:" — select Contacts Only or Everyone.
4) Once everything's set, you're all ready to send or receive files in a flash — no cords, no emails, just pure Apple magic.

CHAPTER TWO

HOW TO USE AIRDROP TO TRANSFER FILES BETWEEN MACS

AirDrop is one of those Apple features that feels like magic when it works—and it usually does! It's a fast and wireless way to share everything from photos to documents between Apple devices, including from one Mac to another. If you've never used it before or just want a refresher, here's how to get started.

Make Sure AirDrop is enabled.

Before sending anything, you'll need to turn on AirDrop on both Macs.

1) Open Finder, and then click AirDrop from the sidebar.

   You can also use Spotlight Search (press Command + Space) and type in "AirDrop."

2) At the bottom of the AirDrop window, you'll see "Allow me to be discovered by" with a dropdown. Click it and choose either Contact Only (recommended for privacy) or Everyone (useful

in public settings if you're not seeing the other device).

3) Once enabled, your Mac will start looking for nearby AirDrop-compatible devices.

Drag and Drop Files to Send

1) With the AirDrop window open, open a second Finder window (Right-click or two-finger click the Finder icon and choose New Finder Window).

2) Find the file you want to send and simply drag it over the device name in the AirDrop window. When the icon highlights, release the file—it'll transfer instantly.

Tip: Got the file on your desktop? No problem—just drag it straight into the AirDrop window.

Share with a Right-Click

Not a fan of dragging files around? You can also send files in just a couple of clicks.

1) Find your file in Finder and right-click (or two-finger click) it.

2) Hover over Share, then select AirDrop.

3) A new window will show nearby devices. Click the one you want, and you're good to go!

AirDrop from an Open File

Many apps let you share directly from within the file itself. If you're working in Preview, for instance, look for the Share button—a little square with an arrow pointing up, usually at the top of the window.

In QuickTime Player? You'll find that same Share icon tucked into the playback controls. Just click it and choose AirDrop.

That's it! Whether you're moving a few photos or a big document, AirDrop is one of the easiest and fastest ways to transfer files between Macs.

Looking to share your screen or stream media instead? You might want to check out AirPlay—another awesome Apple feature that pairs perfectly with AirDrop.

HOW TO ACCESS THE NOTIFICATION CENTER ON MAC

If you're new to macOS or just haven't explored the Notification Center, you're in for a treat. It's been around for a while, but it has evolved significantly in recent versions, offering a centralized space not only for notifications but also for widgets—little at-a-glance summaries of app activities. Whether you're looking to stay on top of app alerts or get real-time info via widgets, knowing how to access and use the Notification Center can seriously enhance your Mac experience. Here's how to find and use it!

What is the Notification Center on Mac?

As the name implies, the Notification Center is your Mac's home base for all notifications. Whenever an app on your Mac needs to alert you about something, whether it's a new email, a calendar reminder, or a weather update, the Notification Center is where those notifications live. Plus, it's home to widgets, which are mini dashboards displaying real-time information from your apps (think of them as app shortcuts with useful data).

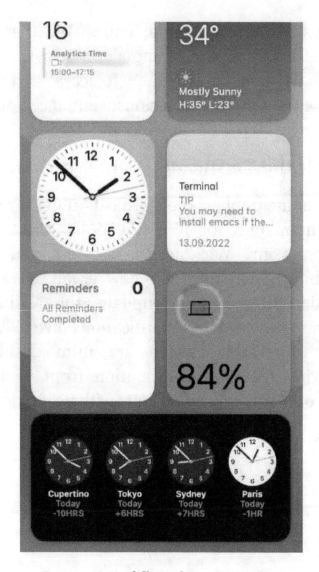

How to Open Notification Center on Your Mac

Getting to Notification Center is easy and there are several ways to do it:

1) Click the Date & Time in the Menu Bar: The quickest way to open it is by clicking the time and date at the top right of your screen. This will reveal a panel with your notifications and widgets.
2) Swipe Left with Your Trackpad: If you're using a trackpad, swipe left from the right edge. This will slide out Notification Center, so you can quickly see your notifications and widgets.

How to Take Control of Your Mac's Performance

Notification Center is useful for managing notifications and widgets, but did you know that you can also use it to optimize your Mac's performance? Many background processes, login items, and launch agents can slow down your system, but you can manage them easily. Apps like CleanMyMac let you identify resource-hogging apps, disable unnecessary startup items, and speed up your system without breaking a sweat. A free trial is available if you're interested in giving it a shot.

How to Manage Notifications in the Notification Center

The beauty of the Notification Center lies in its customization options. You don't have to settle for the default settings—here's how to fine-tune your notifications:

1) Open System Settings: Start by clicking the Apple menu and selecting System Settings.
2) Navigate to Notifications: In the System Settings window, go to Notifications.
3) Customize Individual App Notifications: You'll see a list of apps that can send notifications. For each one, you can control how and where notifications appear. For example, you can choose to show notifications in the Notification Center, mute them entirely, or choose how alert banners and previews behave.

How to Add or Remove Widgets in the Notification Center

Widgets are an incredible feature of macOS, and with the recent updates, you can not only use them within the Notification Center but also place them directly on your desktop. Here's how to manage widgets:

1) Open Notification Center: Click the date and time in the menu bar to open Notification Center.
2) Access Widget Editing: Scroll down and click Edit Widgets at the bottom. Here, you'll see all the widgets available for you to add.
3) Remove Widgets: Widgets that are already added to your Notification Center will have a minus sign (-) in the top-left corner. Click it to remove them.

4) Add New Widgets: At the bottom of the screen, you'll find a widget gallery. To add a widget, simply drag it to the top-right corner of the screen. You can also click the + symbol to add a widget to your Notification Center.
5) Arrange Widgets: Once added, you can reposition widgets by dragging them up or down.
6) Move Widgets to Your Desktop: If you want a widget on your desktop instead of inside the Notification Center, just drag it from the gallery to your desktop and place it wherever you like.
7) Finish Editing: When you're done, click Done at the bottom right of the widget gallery.

How to Manage Widgets in the Notification Center

After adding widgets to the Notification Center, you can edit, remove, or resize them with just a few clicks:

1) Remove a Widget: Open Notification Center, right-click (Control-click) on the widget, and choose Remove Widget.
2) Edit a Widget: Some widgets allow you to edit the content they display. Right-click on the widget and select Edit Widget if the option is available.
3) Resize a Widget: To change the size of a widget, Control-click it and select a different size (small, medium, or large).
4) Done Editing: Once you've customized your widgets to your liking, click Done to save your changes.

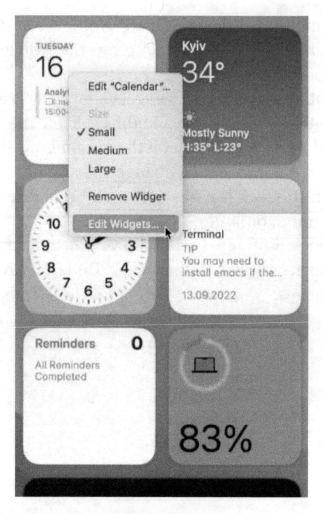

How to Change Widget Settings

For more fine-tuned control over widgets, go to System Settings > Desktop & Dock and scroll down to Widgets. Here, you can adjust:

1) Widget Display: Choose where you want widgets to appear—either in the Notification Center or directly on the desktop.
2) Widget Style: Customize the visual style of the widgets to match your preferences.

Why You'll Love Notification Center

With its combination of notifications and interactive widgets, the Notification Center has become far more than just a passive info hub. It's a powerful tool for staying organized, managing tasks, and accessing useful app data quickly. Whether you're customizing your notifications or adding widgets to your desktop, Notification Center makes your Mac experience smoother and more productive. Explore the features above, and you'll quickly find how easy it is to make this part of macOS work for you!

HOW TO YOUR MAC'S DOCK

One of the most versatile tools on your Mac is the Dock. Not only is it a convenient way to launch your apps, but it can also help you organize your workspace, quickly access files, and even improve your productivity. Whether you're a casual user or a power user, the Dock is here to make your Mac experience smoother and more efficient. Let's explore the many features and customization options that can turn your Dock into a productivity powerhouse.

What's in Your Dock?

By default, the Dock is divided into sections with handy dividers, each serving a different purpose. The leftmost part holds apps that you've either installed or chosen to keep there. Next, you'll find a separator followed by running apps and any apps that you've recently used. To the right, you can place folders, files, and even minimized windows. And, of course, there's the Trash, sitting pretty at the far end.

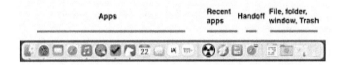

If you want to add a recent app to the Dock, just go to System Preferences > Dock & Menu Bar and enable the "Show recent applications in Dock" option. This is great for keeping your workflow dynamic without cluttering your Dock with icons you don't need all the time.

But wait—there's more! If you've got another Mac nearby and it has an app open that can be handed off to your current device, it'll show up in your Dock as well. A small icon will appear on the app, like Safari in the screenshot above. Click it, and the same page opens up on your Mac.

Customize Your Dock's Position

Most of the time, your Dock sits comfortably at the bottom of your screen, but did you know you can move it? Open System Preferences and click Dock & Menu Bar to change its position. You can switch it to either the left or right side of the screen. Moving it to the side might make your windows feel less cramped and help you use your display's full height.

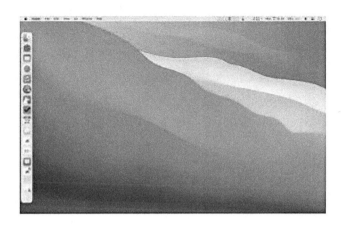

Hide the Dock When You Don't Need It

If you love a clean workspace, consider setting your Dock to hide automatically. Go to Dock & Menu Bar preferences, check automatically hide and show the Dock, and voilà—your Dock will only appear when you hover your cursor over its position. This gives you more screen real estate and lets you focus on the task at hand. Once you move your cursor away, the Dock vanishes until you need it again.

Resize and Magnify Your Dock

Want to make your Dock icons bigger or smaller? You can easily adjust its size. In Dock & Menu Bar preferences, drag the Size slider to your liking. Keep in mind, that the Dock will still adjust its size to fit all your icons if it becomes too crowded. Play around with it to find the size that works best for you.

If you're into some visual flair, try enabling the Magnification feature. This makes icons grow when you hover your cursor over them. It's great for easily spotting apps, but it can be a bit distracting for some users, so give it a go and see what you think!

Add and Remove Items from the Dock

Over time, you might want to tidy up your Dock to keep it focused on your most-used apps. Removing an app is simple: just drag it out of the Dock, and once it's far enough away, a "Remove" label will appear—let go, and it's gone. You can also right-click an icon, then select Options > Remove from Dock if magnification is turned on.

To add apps or files, just drag them to the Dock. You can also change the order of items by dragging them around. For apps that you use often but don't always have open, right-click on an app icon and choose Options > Keep in Dock to make it a permanent fixture.

Animate Your Dock for Extra Fun

If you like a little movement, macOS lets you customize how your Dock items animate. In Dock preferences, you can choose between the Genie Effect (a fun shrinking animation) and the Scale Effect (which resizes the window smoothly). You can even opt to have apps bounce when launched or show a small indicator below an open app's icon, making it easy to spot what's running.

Control Apps Directly from the Dock

Your Dock isn't just for launching apps; it can also serve as a control hub for some apps. For example, in Music, you can click and hold the icon to play, skip tracks, shuffle, or repeat songs. In the Mail, you can compose a new message right from the Dock. If you ever need to quit an app, simply click and hold its icon, then select Quit. If it's unresponsive, hold the Option key and click again to access the Force Quit option.

The Dock is not only functional but it's also packed with small customizations that can boost your workflow. For instance, you can set apps to launch automatically at login, show them in the Finder, or even assign them to a specific desktop using Space.

With just a few tweaks, the Dock becomes more than a taskbar—it becomes a central hub for everything you do on your Mac.

Tip: For those who love to dive deep into macOS, there are hidden preferences in Terminal that let you unlock even more ways to customize the Dock. Who knew the Dock could be so powerful?

With all these tips, you'll find that the Dock can do a lot more than just house icons. It's a key part of your macOS experience and with some fine-tuning; it can help you work faster, stay organized, and look cool while doing it.

CHAPTER THREE

HOW TO CREATE AN APPLE ID ON A MAC

An Apple ID is your all-access pass to everything in the Apple ecosystem—from downloading apps on the App Store and streaming music on Apple Music to syncing content with iCloud and using Find My. It's also essential for purchases, device security, and seamless integration across all your Apple devices.

Whether you're new to Apple or setting up a fresh account, creating an Apple ID is completely free and super easy. Here's how you can do it right from your Mac.

1) Create an Apple ID via System Settings
2) Open System Settings (formerly System Preferences).

3) If no one is signed in, you'll see a blank profile interface—click "Sign In."

At the bottom of the sign-in window, choose "Create Apple ID..."

4) Follow the on-screen instructions to set up your account.

You'll be asked to enter:

a) Your full name
b) Date of birth
c) Country or region
d) A secure password

Answers to security questions for added account protection

After you've completed the form, Apple will send a verification email to the address you used. Once confirmed, that email becomes your official Apple ID.

Create an Apple ID from the Mac App Store

Prefer to go through the App Store? Here's how:

1) Open the Mac App Store.
2) Scroll to the bottom and click "Sign In."
3) Choose "Create Apple ID."
4) You'll need to provide:
    a) Your email address
    b) A strong password
    c) Your country or region

Agreement to Apple's terms and conditions

Tip: You may be asked for billing info, but you can select "None" if you don't want to add a credit card right away.

Sign Up Online Using a Web Browser

You can also create an Apple ID directly on the web:

1) Open Safari or any browser.
2) Go to Apple's official Apple ID page.
3) Scroll down and click "Create your Apple ID."

4) Fill out the form with your info and follow the instructions.

This method works just like the ones in System Settings or the App Store and also includes the email verification step.

No matter which method you choose, you'll be ready to access all of Apple's services with your new ID in just a few minutes.

HOW TO SET UP AND USE ICLOUD DRIVE ON YOUR MAC

Think of iCloud Drive as Apple's take on cloud storage—like Dropbox, but seamlessly integrated with your Apple devices. With iCloud Drive, you can access your files, documents, and folders from your Mac, iPhone, iPad, or even a Windows PC. Whether you're saving work files, personal documents, or random downloads, iCloud Drive keeps everything synced and ready when you need it.

Here's a quick and easy guide to setting it up and using it on your Mac or from the web.

How to Turn On iCloud Drive on a Mac

Haven't enabled iCloud Drive yet? No worries—getting it set up only takes a minute:

1) Click the Apple menu (□) in the top-left corner of your screen.
2) Select System Settings.
3) Tap your Apple ID at the top of the sidebar.
4) Find iCloud Drive and switch it on.

That's it! Once it's enabled, your Mac will automatically begin syncing supported files and folders with iCloud.

How to Access iCloud Drive from Any Web Browser

No Mac handy? You can still get to all your files from any device with internet access.

1) Head to iCloud.com in your browser.
2) Log in using your Apple ID email and password.
3) Complete two-factor authentication if asked.
4) Click on iCloud Drive.

From here, you can browse, download, upload, move, or delete files—just like you would from your desktop.

How to Open iCloud Drive in Finder on Your Mac

Prefer the native Mac experience? You can open iCloud Drive directly in Finder:

1) Open Finder.
2) Click Go in the menu bar.
3) Select iCloud Drive from the dropdown.

Or, hit Command + Space to bring up Spotlight and type "iCloud Drive" for a shortcut. Once inside, you can manage files just like you would with any other folder on your Mac.

Want to Turn Off iCloud Drive?

If you ever decide you no longer want iCloud Drive enabled:

1) Open the Apple menu.
2) Go to System Settings.
3) Click on your Apple ID.
4) Toggle iCloud Drive off.

Disabling iCloud Drive may remove cloud-based files from your Mac, so back up anything important first.

Why You Should Be Using iCloud Drive

If you're already in the Apple ecosystem, iCloud Drive is a no-brainer. It keeps your important documents available across all your devices, and it's built right into the apps and tools you already use every day. Once it's set up, it works quietly in the background—just open a folder, drop in a file, and it'll be ready wherever you are.

HOW TO TRANSFER PHOTOS FROM IPHONE TO MACBOOK AIR

Do you have a bunch of great shots on your iPhone and want them on your MacBook Air? Whether you're backing them up, editing them on a bigger screen, or just organizing your digital life, moving photos between devices is super easy—once you know how. Let's walk through the most convenient ways to do it.

1) The Easiest Method: iCloud Photo Sync

If you're all about convenience, iCloud is your best friend. With iCloud Photo syncing, every photo you take on your iPhone magically shows up on your MacBook—no cables, no taps, no extra apps.

Here's how to set it up:

On your iPhone:

a) Open Settings, scroll down, and tap Photos.
b) Toggle on iCloud Photos.

Tip: You can also find the setting via Settings > General > iPhone Storage, then scroll to find iCloud Photos.

On your MacBook Air:

a) Launch the Photos app.
b) If prompted, agree to enable iCloud.
c) If not prompted, go to the menu bar and click Photos > Settings (or Preferences).
d) Navigate to the iCloud tab and check iCloud Photos.

e) Done! Now, whenever you're connected to Wi-Fi, your devices will stay in sync. Just keep in mind: Apple gives you 5GB of free iCloud storage. If your photo library is massive, you may need to upgrade your storage plan.

2) AirDrop: Quick Transfers, No Wires Needed

Want to transfer just a few photos without syncing your whole library? AirDrop is perfect for that. It's quick, easy, and wireless.

Here's how to use AirDrop:

a) Turn on Wi-Fi and Bluetooth on both your iPhone and MacBook.
b) On your iPhone, open the Photos app and go to the album with the photos you want.
c) Tap Select and choose the photos.
d) Tap the Share icon (a box with an upward arrow).
e) Tap AirDrop, then choose your MacBook from the list.
f) On your MacBook, click Accept if prompted.

The photos will appear in your Downloads folder. Simple as that!

3) Use a Lightning Cable for a Direct Transfer

Prefer the old-school, plug-in method? You can use your iPhone's Lightning cable to move photos manually.

Here's how to do it:

a) Connect your iPhone to your MacBook with the charging cable. (You might need a USB-C adapter depending on your Mac model.)
b) Unlock your iPhone and tap Trust This Computer if it pops up.
c) On your MacBook, open the Photos app.
d) Under Devices, click your iPhone.
e) Select the photos you want, then click Import Selected, or click Import All New Items.

The imported images will show up in the Library and Imports sections of the Photos app.

Troubleshooting Tips

Even smooth setups can hit a snag. Here's how to fix common issues:

Is AirDrop not working?

1) Make sure both devices have AirDrop set to Contacts Only or Everyone.

2) Try switching between those settings, toggling Wi-Fi/Bluetooth off and on, or restarting both devices.

Cable connection failing?

1) Unplug and reconnect the cable.
2) Make sure your iPhone is unlocked.
3) Try restarting both your iPhone and MacBook.

iCloud syncing issues?

1) Double-check that iCloud Photos is enabled on both devices.
2) Verify that both are signed into the same Apple ID and connected to Wi-Fi.

No matter your tech comfort level, there's a photo transfer method for you. Whether you prefer the hands-off ease of iCloud, the speed of AirDrop, or the reliability of a wired connection, you'll have your favorite pics on your MacBook Air in no time.

CHAPTER FOUR

HOW TO USE TOUCH ID ON YOUR MAC

Got a Mac with Touch ID? Whether you're using a MacBook Pro with a Touch Bar or one of the sleek new MacBook Air models powered by the M1 chip, Touch ID is a super handy feature you'll want to take advantage of. From unlocking your device to making quick payments, here's how to set it up and get the most out of it.

What Can You Do with Touch ID on a Mac?

Touch ID isn't just about unlocking your Mac—it's a powerful little tool that can streamline your whole experience. With it, you can:

1) Instantly unlock your Mac without typing a password.

2) Approve Apple Pay transactions quickly and securely.
3) Sign in to apps with just your fingerprint.
4) Make purchases on the App Store, iTunes, and Apple Books without typing your Apple ID password.

Where's the Touch ID Sensor?

If you're wondering where the magic happens, the Touch ID sensor is located at the top-right corner of your keyboard—usually on the power button. It's only available on newer MacBooks, so if you're using an iMac, Mac mini, or Mac Pro, you won't have a built-in Touch ID. That said, if you own an Apple Watch, you can still get similar convenience for unlocking and approving some actions.

How to Set Up Touch ID on Your Mac

Setting up Touch ID is quick and painless. Here's how to do it:

1) Click the Apple menu in the top-left corner of your screen.

Select System Preferences, then choose Touch ID.

2) Click Add a Fingerprint.

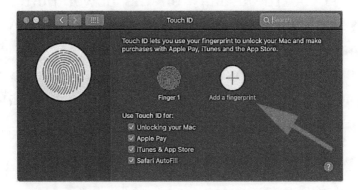

3) Enter your Mac's password when prompted.

4) Follow the on-screen steps to scan your fingerprint.

5) You can add up to three fingerprints per user account—handy if you use different fingers in different situations. Once you're done, click Done to finish setup.

How to Customize How You Use Touch ID

After registering your fingerprint, you'll see several options to choose what Touch ID can be used for:

1) Unlocking your Mac
2) Apple Pay
3) iTunes & App Store purchases
4) Autofill in Safari

Just tick the boxes for the features you want, and you're good to go!

How to Log In with Touch ID

Once everything is set up, waking your Mac from sleep becomes a breeze—just tap the Touch ID sensor with your registered finger. Keep in mind, if your Mac was just restarted or shut down, you'll need to type your password the first time before Touch ID kicks in.

How to Pay with Apple Pay Using Touch ID

This is one of the coolest features of Touch ID on Mac. To enable it:

1) Open System Preferences.
2) Click on Wallet & Apple Pay.
3) Add your card details by following the prompts.

Now, whenever you shop online with Apple Pay, just rest your finger on the Touch ID sensor to confirm the purchase—secure and effortless.

With everything set up, using Touch ID on your Mac becomes second nature. It's a small feature that adds a big boost to both security and convenience.

HOW TO USE STAGE MANAGER ON YOUR MAC

Looking for a smarter way to handle the clutter of open windows on your Mac? Enter Stage Manager — Apple's bold new take on multitasking introduced in macOS 13 Ventura. Love it or hate it, it's a feature worth exploring if you're tired of juggling windows manually.

What is a Stage Manager?

Stage Manager is Apple's sleek attempt to streamline window management. Instead of a chaotic desktop filled with overlapping apps, Stage Manager tucks away unused windows into a side shelf, letting you focus on one group of apps at a time. It's perfect for users who crave a cleaner, more organized workspace.

How to Turn On Stage Manager

1) Click the Control Center icon in the top-right corner of your screen.
2) Look for Stage Manager and toggle it on.
3) That's it! Once enabled, you'll see your current app front and center, with other apps and windows neatly arranged on a side shelf (which can appear on either side, depending on where your Dock is).

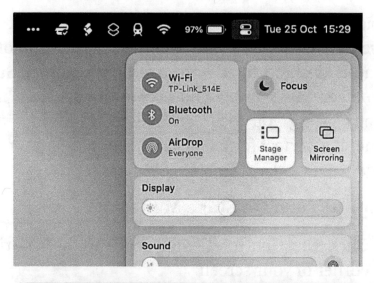

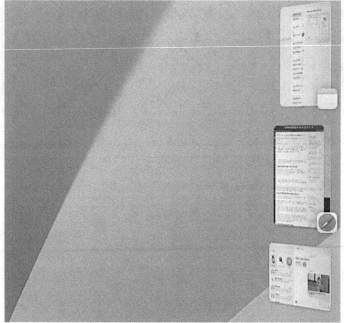

Tips to Get the Most Out of Stage Manager

Switch Apps Easily: Click on any app on the shelf to bring it forward, or use Command + Tab to cycle through them like usual.

Use Gestures: Swipe up with three or four fingers to open Mission Control same as before.

Group Windows for Efficiency: Drag and drop apps together to create custom groups. Perfect for multitasking like having Safari and Notes open side-by-side for research.

Hide the Shelf When Needed: Drag an app window over the shelf to make it disappear temporarily and maximize your screen space.

Manage Multiple Windows: If you have multiple Safari or Finder windows, keep them together in a group, or switch between them using Command + ~ (the tilde key under Esc).

Customize Your View: Go to Settings > Desktop & Dock, click Customize next to Stage Manager, and choose whether to show recent apps, hide the shelf, or display one window at a time.

Who Should Use Stage Manager?

Stage Manager isn't for everyone—but it shines in a few key scenarios:

New Mac users: It helps reduce overwhelm by simplifying how apps appear on the screen.

People who lose windows easily: Grouping Finder windows or keeping communication apps like Slack and Teams together can seriously cut down on window-hunting.

Workflow junkies: If you have go-to app combinations for work, Stage Manager makes switching between them feel seamless.

But if you already use Spaces heavily or rely on third-party window managers like Magnet or Rectangle, Stage Manager might feel a bit redundant.

Stage Manager changes how focus works on macOS. For example, if you switch from a Safari window to a Finder group, your Safari session disappears until you switch back. It can take a little time to get used to that.

Also, your desktop icons will be hidden by default in Stage Manager mode, but you can always click on the desktop or tweak the settings to bring them back.

Is Stage Manager Worth It?

If you're the type who prefers structure over chaos, Stage Manager could quickly become one of your favorite tools. It's not just a cosmetic change—it can boost your productivity once you get the hang of it.

So don't give up after five minutes. Spend a little time learning the flow, customizing the settings, and seeing if it fits into your workflow. You might just find yourself wondering how you ever worked without it.

HOW TO USE THE MAC APP STORE

The Mac App Store is your go-to destination for downloading, updating, and discovering thousands of apps for your Mac. Launched in 2011, this digital storefront is curated by Apple and seamlessly ties into the broader App Store ecosystem used on iPhones and iPads. Whether you're looking for productivity tools, creative software, or the latest games, it's all just a few clicks away.

What Makes the Mac App Store Special?

Unlike open marketplaces, the Mac App Store is fully managed by Apple. That means every app available here has been reviewed and approved for safety and quality. Developers must follow Apple's guidelines (which can change often), but in return, they get access to a global audience and top-notch developer tools.

Every app listing includes detailed info: user ratings, age suitability, supported languages, developer details, file size, and privacy practices. You'll also find screenshots, previews, and "What's New" updates.

Navigating the Mac App Store

The Mac App Store is organized into several easy-to-navigate sections, each tailored to different user interests:

Discover

This is the homepage of the store—where you'll find trending apps, editor's picks, developer spotlights, and top charts for both free and paid apps. See something you like? Just click the app's name to learn more, or hit 'Get' (for free apps) or the price tag to buy and download. If you already own the app, you'll see 'Open' or a cloud icon if it's not currently installed.

How to Search

Know what you're looking for? Use the search bar at the top left to type in keywords or app names. You'll get instant results you can explore, complete with all the info and download options you need.

How to use Arcade

Apple Arcade subscribers can access this tab to explore a curated collection of high-quality games—all ad-free and without in-app purchases. Not a member yet? You can subscribe directly from this page. Games are sorted by popularity, genre, and new releases.

How to Create

This section is all about creativity—think photo editors, video tools, design software, and more. It's perfect for artists, content creators, and anyone who loves to make things. Like other sections, each app includes details, previews, and one-click downloads.

Work

Need tools for productivity or running a business? The Work section is where you'll find Microsoft 365 apps, organization tools, finance trackers, writing assistants, and more. There's also an Editor's Choice spotlight to help you find top-rated picks.

Play

If you're into gaming, this is your hub. The Play section features a wide variety of games—many not available on Apple Arcade. Discover top free titles, paid hits, and editor favorites across genres.

Develop

Targeted at software creators and tech enthusiasts, this smaller section includes development tools and resources. You'll find compilers, text editors, testing tools, and other essential utilities for building apps.

Categories: Browse apps by theme, from Education and Music to Travel and Utilities. There's also a special section for Safari extensions and developer tools.

Updates: Here, you'll see which apps have updates ready to install. Just click 'Update' to stay current.

Your Account

Click your name at the bottom-left of the store to access your account dashboard. Here, you'll see a history of all your purchases, including those not currently installed (which can be re-downloaded anytime). You can also redeem gift cards, manage Family Sharing purchases, and—on Apple Silicon Macs—toggle between Mac and iOS/iPad apps that are cross-compatible.

Preferences & Customization

Want to tweak your experience? Head to the App Store > Preferences menu in the toolbar.

From here, you can:

1) Enable automatic app updates.
2) Sync downloads across devices using the same Apple ID.
3) Auto-play app preview videos.

4) Show or hide app ratings and review tools.

Whether you're a power user, creative professional, gamer, or someone who just wants to stay productive, the Mac App Store has something for everyone. It's safe, constantly updated, and tightly integrated with the rest of Apple's ecosystem—making it one of the easiest and most secure ways to get the apps you need on your Mac.

HOW TO SAFARI ON YOUR MAC

Safari is your go-to browser on Mac—fast, sleek, and built by Apple. Whether you're diving into a research project, hunting down memes, or just browsing for fun, Safari is the gateway to it all. Let's walk through the essentials to get you up and running like a pro.

How to Visit a Website

Need to jump to a specific site? If you know the URL (like www.apple.com), here's how to go straight there:

1) Open Safari (you'll find it in the Dock or your Applications folder).
2) Click the address bar at the top—it'll highlight.
3) Type in the website address.

4) Press Return and boom—you're there!

How to Search the Web from the Address Bar

Don't have a specific site in mind? No problem—you can search right from the address bar:

1) Launch Safari.
2) Click the address bar.
3) Type your search, like "funny cat videos".
4) Hit Return—you'll be taken to Google (or your default search engine) with all the results waiting.

How to Bookmark a Website

Found something you love and want to save it for later? Time to bookmark:

1) With Safari open, go to the page you want to save.
2) Press Command + D.
3) Give it a name if you like, or keep the default.
4) Click Add or press Return.

Tip: To keep bookmarks one click away, go to the View menu at the top and choose Show Favorites Bar. Your top sites will appear just under the address bar—super handy!

How to View All Your Bookmarks

Prefer keeping things organized? Here's how to see every bookmark you've saved:

1) Open Safari.
2) Click the Show Sidebar button (next to the address bar).
3) Tap the Bookmarks tab (it looks like a little book).

Now you can browse all your folders and saved pages in one place.

How to Remove a Bookmark

Tidy up your bookmarks when you don't need them anymore:

1) Open Safari.
2) From the menu bar at the top, click Bookmarks, then choose Edit Bookmarks.
3) Click the arrow next to Favorites to expand the list.
4) Right-click (or hold Control and click) the one you want to delete.
5) Select Delete—and it's gone.

How to Add a Page to Your Reading List

Want to save an article or story for later? Add it to your Reading List—it even works offline!

1) Visit the site you want to save.
2) Press Shift + Command + D, or go to Bookmarks > Add to Reading List in the menu bar.
3) You'll see a little animation as it slides over to the sidebar—nice touch!

How to View Your Reading List

Ready to catch up on your saved reads?

1) Open Safari.
2) Click the Show Sidebar button.
3) Click the tab with the glasses icon—that's your Reading List.
4) Just click on any item to read it.

How to Remove Items from Your Reading List

Clearing out your list is just as easy:

1) In Safari, click the Show Sidebar button.
2) Head to the Reading List tab (glasses icon).
3) Right-click (or Control-click) the item you're done with.
4) Choose Remove Item.

And that's it! You're officially on your way to becoming a Safari-savvy Mac user. Whether you're organizing bookmarks or saving stories to read offline, Safari's got tools to keep your web experience smooth and easy.

Safari Tips

Whether you're planning a surprise gift or just want a cleaner, more private browsing experience, Safari on Mac is packed with powerful features to explore the web your way. Here's how to get the most out of it:

Go Incognito with Private Browsing

Need to keep your browsing under wraps? Private Browsing mode is your go-to. It doesn't save your history, AutoFill data, or cookies — perfect for gift shopping or, you know... whatever you're up to.

How to enable it:

1) Open Safari from your Dock or Finder.
2) Go to the File menu at the top-left.
3) Click New Private Window, or just press Shift + Command + N.

Boom — you're browsing incognito. Safari won't remember the pages you visit or any login details.

Check a Website's Privacy Report

With macOS Big Sur and later, Safari helps you see who's trying to follow your trail.

1) To view the Privacy Report:
2) Launch Safari and head to any site.
3) Click the Privacy Report icon next to the address bar.
4) Hit the info (**i**☐) icon to see a full list of blocked trackers.
5) Click the red close button when you're done snooping around.

How to Enhance Safari with Extensions

Safari extensions let you customize your browser — block ads, boost productivity, or connect with your favorite apps.

To install extensions:

1) Open Safari.
2) Click Safari in the menu bar, then select Safari Extensions.
3) You'll be taken to the Mac App Store. Browse, download, and install like any other app.
4) Open the extension's app to activate it in Safari.

Extensions are free, but the service they work with might not be.

How to Pin Your Favorite Tabs

Keep your go-to websites just a click away with pinned tabs — no more hunting them down!

Here's how:

1) Open Safari and click View > Show Tab Bar (if it's not already showing).
2) Visit a site you love.
3) Drag the tab to the left until it shrinks into an icon.
4) To unpin it, just drag it back to the right.

Set Your Homepage

Tired of landing on apple.com every time you open Safari? Change it up!

To set your homepage:

1) Go to Safari > Preferences and stay on the General tab.
2) Enter your favorite site next to Homepage or click Set to Current Page.
3) Choose Homepage from the drop-down menus next to "New windows open with" and "New tabs open with."

How to Personalize Your Start Page

macOS Big Sur and later lets you turn your start page into a dashboard of your favorites.

Here's how to customize it:

1) Open Safari (you'll land on the start page unless it's been changed).
2) Click the settings icon in the bottom-right corner.
3) Select or deselect what you want to show — like Reading List, Siri Suggestions, or your Privacy Report.
4) Add some flair with a custom background image!

Share What You Discover

Found something worth sharing? Safari makes it easy.

To share a webpage:

1) Visit the site.
2) Click the Share button (a square with an arrow) in the toolbar.
3) Pick how you want to send it — Messages, Mail, AirDrop, Notes, and more.

Use Reader View for a Clean Read

Don't let clutter get in the way of a good article. Reader View clears distractions so you can focus on the words.

To activate it:

1) Visit a compatible webpage.
2) Click the Reader View button — the four horizontal lines on the left of the address bar.

How to Customize Reader View

Once you're in Reader View, why not tweak it to your style?

Change Background Color:

1) Click the Reader Options button (the two As on the right).
2) Pick the color that's easiest on your eyes.
3) Change the Font:

   Same Reader Options menu — select the font you prefer.

4) Adjust Text Size:

   Use the smaller "A" to shrink the text or the bigger "A" to increase it.

CHAPTER FIVE

HOW TO USE "HEY SIRI" HANDS-FREE ON YOUR MAC

You might already know that Apple's "Hey Siri" feature lets you interact with your devices using just your voice—no hands required. It's already a staple on recent Apple gadgets like the fifth-gen iPad mini, third-gen iPad Air, and second-gen AirPods. But did you know your Mac can get in on the action too?

That's right—many of Apple's newer Mac models now support "Hey Siri" completely hands-free. No need to click a menu bar icon or hit a keyboard shortcut. Just speak up, and Siri is ready to help.

Which Macs Support Hands-Free "Hey Siri"

If you've got a newer Mac with Apple's T2 security chip, you're likely good to go. This includes a range of MacBook Pro, MacBook Air, and iMac models released in recent years. And as Apple continues to roll out updates, expect this feature to become even more widespread.

How to Turn On "Hey Siri" on Your Mac

Here's how to set it up and start using Siri without lifting a finger:

1) Click the Apple menu in the top-left corner of your screen and select System Preferences.
2) Choose Siri from the list of options.
3) Check the box next to "Listen for 'Hey Siri'".

4) Click Continue, then follow the on-screen prompts to train Siri to recognize your voice.
5) Once you're done, click done, and close the System Preferences window.

Now you're all set! Just say "Hey Siri" and start talking—ask a question, set a reminder, send a message, or anything else Siri can help with. If you've used Siri on an iPhone or iPad, you'll feel right at home.

HOW TO USE STACKS AND QUICK LOOK

macOS Ventura comes packed with features that streamline your workflow, and two of the most useful ones in Finder are Stacks and Quick Look. These tools help you stay organized and give you lightning-fast previews of your files—perfect for multitasking and staying efficient.

Stacks is A Cleaner, Smarter Desktop

Stacks help tame a messy desktop by organizing your files into neat groups. Think of them as spring-loaded folders that pop open when you click them. You can group Stacks by file type, date, or tags, and use them both on the Desktop and in the Dock.

How to Use Stacks in the Dock

To set up a Stack in your Dock:

1) Drag a folder from Finder into the right side of the Dock (just to the left of the Trash).

2) Control-click (or right-click) the folder icon in the Dock to customize it.
3) From the popup menu, choose:
4) "Display as" → "Stack"
5) "View content as" → Choose between Fan, Grid, List, or Automatic
6) "Sort by" → Organize by Name, Date, or Kind

'Once it's set, just click the Stack in the Dock and it will fan out or display in the view you selected. Click any item to open it instantly. Pro tip: You must click the icon, not the file name, to open it!

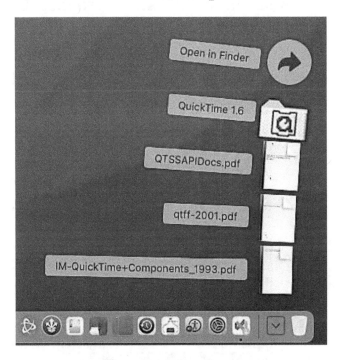

How to use stacks on the Desktop

Want a cleaner desktop without manually dragging things around?

1) Control-click (or right-click) anywhere on your Desktop.
2) Select "Use Stacks" from the menu.

3) Finder will group your files—usually by type—into tidy icon stacks. Clicking a Stack reveals its contents, just like in the Dock.

You can tweak how Stacks are grouped by right-clicking the Desktop again and using the "Sort By" menu. Or, go to View → Show View Options in the Finder menu bar and use the "Stack By" setting to sort by Kind, Dates, or Tags.

Heads up: Turning on Stacks will rearrange your Desktop, and disabling it doesn't always restore your original layout. Consider DE cluttering first.

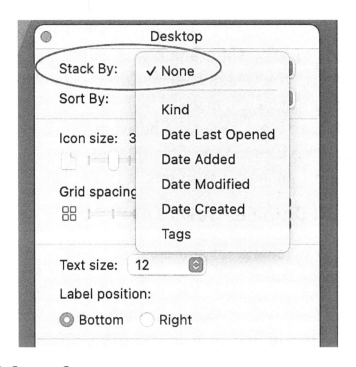

Quick Look

Quick Look is one of macOS's most underrated power tools. With a single tap of the spacebar, you can peek inside nearly any file without opening a full app.

How to Use Quick Look

1) Select one or more files in Finder.
2) Tap the spacebar.
3) A preview window appears showing the selected file. Use the left/right arrows in the top-left to cycle through multiple files.

4) You can resize the window, go full screen, and even view a thumbnail grid (upper-right grid icon) if you've selected multiple files. From this preview, you can also:
    a) Share files using the Share button
    b) Open files in their default apps
    c) Edit images or trim media (more below!)

Image Editing in Quick Look

When previewing an image, you'll see tools in the top-right corner:

1) Rotate the image 90° with each click
2) Edit the image with markup tools (draw, crop, adjust)
3) Click Done to save your changes.

If the image contains text, look for a small button in the bottom right. Click it to extract text using macOS's built-in AI. Then hit "Copy All" to grab the text and paste it anywhere.

How to use PDFs and Text Files

When previewing PDFs or text files, Quick Look displays a scrollable view and a thumbnail sidebar. Click any thumbnail to jump to that page—super handy for skimming documents.

Audio & Video Files

Quick Look includes playback controls for audio and video. You can even do basic trimming:

1) Click the Trim button (top-right)
2) Adjust start/end points visually
3) Save the changes right from the preview
4) Special File Types

Quick Look can preview some unique file types too:

Unknown files or folders – Shows basic info like name, size, and last modified date.

Quick Look in Third-Party Apps

Apple provides a Quick Look API, which means developers can integrate the feature into their apps. However, it's up to them to add support—so not every third-party app includes Quick Look previews by default.

Whether you're DE cluttering your workspace with Stacks or breezing through files with Quick Look, these built-in tools can seriously boost your productivity on macOS Ventura. Give them a try and see how much faster your workflow becomes!

HOW TO CREATE A NEW FOLDER ON YOUR MAC

Whether you're saving photos, text files, or video clips, organizing them on your Mac can make your digital life a whole lot easier. As your collection of files grows, it can become overwhelming to locate what you need—fast. That's where folders come in. Just like traditional file folders, they help keep your Mac tidy and efficient by grouping related files. You can even sort files within a folder based on your preferences.

How to Create a New Folder on macOS

No matter how you like to work, macOS offers multiple ways to create a folder. Try each one to find what feels most natural for your workflow:

1) Using the Menu Bar
   a) Navigate to your Mac desktop.
   b) Make sure you're in "Finder" mode (click any blank space on the desktop if you're not).
   c) In the top-left menu bar, click File > New Folder.
   d) Voilà! A new untitled folder will appear on your desktop.

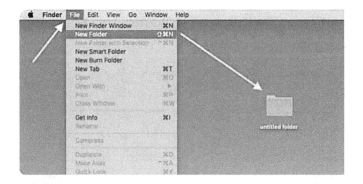

2) Right-Click Method

a) Head to the desktop.

b) Right-click on an empty area (or tap with two fingers on a MacBook trackpad).

c) Select New Folder from the context menu.

d) A new folder should pop up right away.

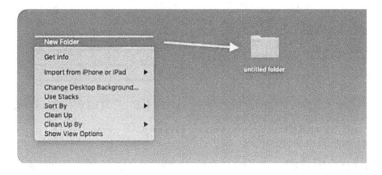

3) Keyboard Shortcut

a) While on your desktop, press Command (⌘) + Shift + N.

b) A brand-new folder will appear in seconds.

Tip: Keyboard shortcuts are a fast and efficient way to speed up your workflow. Get used to using them and you'll be flying through file management tasks in no time.

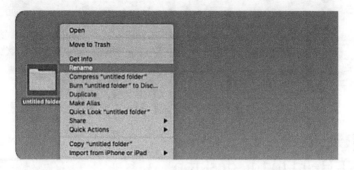

How to Rename, Organize, and Manage Your Folders

Once you've created your folder, it's time to name it:

1) Double-click the folder name to highlight it and type your new name.
2) Or, right-click the folder and select rename from the dropdown menu.
3) You can rename folders as often as needed, which is handy as your projects evolve.

Adding Files

To add items to your folder:

1) Drag and drop the files into the folder icon until it is highlighted in blue.
2) Alternatively, open the folder and drag files directly into the window.

3) You can even create subfolders inside a main folder using any of the three methods above.

Deleting Folders or Files

1) Drag any unwanted folder or file into the Trash on your Dock.
2) Or right-click the item and choose Move to Trash.

Accidentally delete something? Don't worry—your files can usually be recovered from the Trash or through Time Machine backups.

Tips for Folder Security and Performance

If your Mac starts feeling sluggish, clutter could be the culprit. Too many files and folders on the desktop can slow things down. Consider moving larger or less-used files to a cloud service like HiDrive from IONOS for extra space and security.

Want to Keep Your Data Safe?

Use encryption to password-protect sensitive folders on your Mac.

Back up your important data regularly to avoid accidental loss or corruption.

Tip: Services like MyDefender from IONOS can help automate your backups and store them in ISO-certified data centers for top-level protection.

By staying organized with folders and leveraging the built-in tools on macOS, you'll streamline your digital workspace and keep your files secure, searchable, and safely stored.

HOW TO USE SYSTEM PREFERENCES ON YOUR MAC

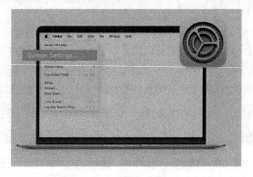

If you're using a Mac, you've got access to one of the most powerful customization hubs built into any computer: System Preferences—now known as System Settings in macOS Ventura and Sonoma. This is your Mac's control center, where you can fine-tune everything from your desktop background to your Wi-Fi and privacy settings. Want to tailor your Mac to match your style and workflow? This is where the magic happens.

In this guide, we'll show you how to quickly find System Preferences (or System Settings) on your Mac and how to start using it like a pro.

What is System Preferences (or System Settings)?

Every operating system has a central place where users can tweak how things look and behave. In Windows, that's the Control Panel or Settings app. On macOS, that hub is System Preferences—or System Settings in newer versions.

This is where you control things like your internet connection, user accounts, sound, notifications, and more. If there's something about your Mac you want to change, chances are you'll do it here.

Where to Find System Preferences on a Mac

Can't locate it? No worries—here are a few easy ways to open it:

1) Via the Apple Menu
2) Click the Apple logo in the top-left corner of your screen.
3) On macOS Ventura or later: Choose System Settings.
4) On older versions: Choose System Preferences.

Via Finder

1) Open Finder (the smiling blue face icon).
2) Select Applications from the sidebar.
3) Scroll down and double-click System Preferences or System Settings.

Via the Dock

Look for the gear icon in your Dock. That's your shortcut to System Preferences/Settings. Click it to dive in.

Tip: Want to keep your Dock tidy and efficient? Apps like Almighty let you group icons by type, frequency, or custom categories—and even add visual spacers for better organization.

How to Use System Settings Like a Pro

Despite how comprehensive it is, the interface is super straightforward. You'll find a scrollable sidebar on the left—each category opens into its own set of options.

Here are a few useful areas to explore:

1) General > Software Update – Keep your Mac up to date.
2) Users & Groups – Add or manage users.

3) Apple ID – Manage your iCloud, App Store, and Apple services.
4) Wi-Fi – Connect to and manage wireless networks.
5) Bluetooth – Pair wireless devices like headphones or keyboards.
6) Notifications – Choose how and when apps can notify you.
7) Time Machine – Set up backups to protect your data.

And that's just the start!

Troubleshooting or Boosting Performance?

Many users open System Settings because something's acting up. If that's you, you might want to skip the digging and go straight to a utility like CleanMyMac.

Here's how it helps:

1) Open CleanMyMac.
2) Click Performance > Run.
3) Under Maintenance Tasks, check off things like:
4) Flush DNS Cache
5) Reindex Spotlight
6) Repair Disk Permissions
7) Click Run and let it do the heavy lifting.

It's a great way to give your Mac a fresh start without having to dig into dozens of settings yourself.

How to Search Within System Settings

Not sure where a particular setting lives? Just use the search bar at the top of the System Settings window. Type in a keyword and your Mac will guide you to the right place instantly.

What if System Preferences Aren't Responding?

Occasionally, the System Preferences app might freeze or stop opening properly. If that happens, try these quick fixes:

1) Force Quit & Relaunch
2) Click the Apple menu > Force Quit
3) Select System Preferences and click Force Quit
4) Restart Your Mac
5) Update macOS – Sometimes bugs are fixed with a simple software update.

By learning how to use System Preferences (or System Settings), you're unlocking the full potential of your Mac. Whether you're customizing your setup or solving issues under the hood, it all starts here.

CHAPTER SIX

HOW TO CHANGE THE SCREEN SAVER ON YOUR MAC

Want to give your Mac a personal touch or just protect your screen from burn-in? Whether you're into sleek visuals or fun photo slideshows, macOS makes it easy to customize your screen saver. Here's how to set it up—and why it's worth doing.

Why Use a Screen Saver?

Some older or specialty displays—like OLED, plasma, or CRT—can suffer from burn-in, where static images left on the screen too long leave a permanent mark. That's where screen savers come in: they keep things moving to help avoid those unwanted ghost images. Even if you're using a modern LCD screen that's not prone to burn-in, screen savers can still add some charm to your desktop.

From soothing visuals to custom messages or slideshows of your favorite memories, screen savers offer a nice way to express your style when you're away from your Mac.

If you're stepping away for an extended time, it might be even better to have your Mac turn off the display or go to sleep—that saves power while still protecting your screen.

How to Set Up a Screen Saver on macOS

Getting started is simple:

1) Click the Apple logo in the top-left corner of your screen and select System Preferences (or System Settings on newer versions of macOS).

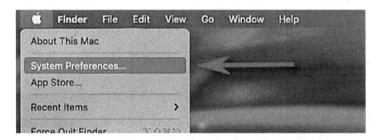

2) In the window that opens, click Desktop & Screen Saver.

3) At the top, switch to the Screen Saver tab.

4) Here, you'll see a lineup of available screen savers on the left. Click through the list to see a live preview of each one on the right side. Once you find one you like, select it.

Customize Your Screen Saver Experience

You can tailor how and when your screen saver kicks in:

1) Use the "Start after" dropdown to choose how long your Mac should wait before activating the screen saver (e.g., 5 minutes of inactivity).
2) Want to mix it up? Check the box for "Random screen saver" so it rotates through different ones.
3) You can also toggle the clock display to show the time while the screen saver is running.

Want a quick way to trigger it manually? Click Hot Corners and assign one of your screen's corners to launch the screen saver when you move your cursor there.

Once you've made your choices, just close the System Preferences window—your settings are saved automatically. If you ever change your mind and want to turn the screen saver off, just head back to the same place and uncheck "Show screen saver after".

HOW TO USE GENMOJI TO THE MAC

With the macOS Sequoia 15.3 beta, Apple is bringing a splash of creativity to the Mac by introducing Genmoji — custom, AI-generated emojis that Mac users can create with just a simple text prompt. This fun feature first debuted with iOS 18.2 and iPadOS 18.2, but until now, it hasn't made its way to macOS.

Now available on all Macs powered by Apple silicon, Genmoji acts just like regular emojis on devices running iOS 18.1, iPadOS 18.1, macOS Sequoia 15.1, and newer. On older Apple devices or Android platforms, they'll appear as images instead — still cool, just not quite as dynamic.

Creating Genmoji is easy. Just open the emoji picker — you can do that with the Control + Command + Space shortcut in apps like Notes, or by clicking the emoji button in Messages. From there, you'll be able to generate a unique emoji character based on your prompt, right from your Mac.

Even better? All Genmoji magic happens directly on your device thanks to Apple Intelligence, keeping everything fast, smooth, and private.

HOW TO COPY AND PASTE ON A MAC

If you're switching from a Windows PC to a Mac, you might find yourself momentarily puzzled by the new keyboard layout and shortcuts. Don't worry— while macOS might look and feel a little different at first, most everyday tasks (like copying and pasting) are just as easy once you get the hang of them.

Here's how to copy and paste text and images on your Mac, step by step.

How to Copy and Paste Text on a Mac

1) Highlight the Text
   a) Select the text you want to copy.
   b) You can click and drag your mouse over the desired section to highlight it, or click at the start (or end) of the text, hold down Shift, and use your arrow keys to expand the selection.
2) Copy the Text
   a) With the text selected, press Command (⌘) + C to copy it.

    b) Alternatively, right-click on the highlighted area (or hold Control and click) to bring up a menu, then choose Copy.

3) Choose Where to Paste

Click on the spot where you want to paste the text—this could be a search bar, message field, or any editable area.

4) Paste the Text

    a) Press Command ($\mathcal{H}$) + V to paste it.

    b) Prefer to match the style of the destination text? Use Option + Shift + Command + V instead, and your copied text will blend right in.

Need to cut instead of copy? Just press Command ($\mathcal{H}$) + X to remove the text and save it to your clipboard, ready to paste somewhere else.

Copying and Pasting Images on a Mac

1) Select the Image

Find the image you want to copy. Right-click on it, or hold Control and click to bring up the options menu.

2) Copy the Image

From the dropdown menu, select Copy Image.

3) Choose Your Destination

Click in the spot where you want the image to go—this could be inside a document, email, or image editor.

4) Paste the Image

Press Command (⌘) + V, or right-click (Control-click) again and choose Paste. Your image will appear right where you want it.

Once you've practiced these shortcuts a few times, they'll become second nature. Whether you're working on documents, sending emails, or editing images, knowing how to copy and paste efficiently is a fundamental Mac skill that saves time and effort.

HOW TO USE FACETIME ON A MAC

Can't always be with your loved ones in person? No worries—FaceTime lets you stay visually connected with family and friends, no matter the distance. Whether you're planning a video chat or just want to hear someone's voice, FaceTime is a fantastic, free way to keep in touch—as long as everyone's got an Apple device.

You'll learn how to make FaceTime calls from your Mac, set it up for incoming calls, tweak some settings, and pick up some helpful tips along the way.

Why FaceTime?

One of the biggest perks of FaceTime is that it's completely free. It doesn't use your call minutes—it runs over Wi-Fi or your data connection. That means even if someone's out and about, they can still chat with you without racking up extra charges (as long as they have enough data).

Not in the mood for a video call? No problem—FaceTime also offers high-quality audio-only calls, which often sound clearer than regular mobile calls.

Who Can You FaceTime?

Here's the catch: FaceTime only works between Apple devices. You'll need an iPhone 4 or newer, an iPad 2 or later, an iPod touch with iOS 4.1+, or a Mac with macOS 10.9.2 or later. The person on the other end also needs to be signed in to FaceTime, and if they're on a Mac, the app must be open.

What You'll Need on Your Mac

To make FaceTime work smoothly on your Mac, here's what you need:

1) A reliable internet connection: Minimum 128 Kbps for standard calls, or 1 Mbps if you want HD.
2) A camera: Most Macs have a built-in FaceTime camera. If you're on a Mac mini or Mac Pro, you may need an external webcam.
3) A microphone: Built-in mics are standard, but a headset with a mic works too.
4) An Apple ID: Required to sign in and make calls.

How to Set Up FaceTime on Your Mac

1) Open the FaceTime app. Use Spotlight (Cmd + Space) and type "FaceTime."
2) Sign in with your Apple ID. Don't have one? You can create one right in the app.
3) Set your contact preferences:

   Click FaceTime > Preferences from the top menu.

4) Choose which emails or numbers you want people to use to reach you.
5) To add or update contact info:
6) Go to System Settings > Apple ID > Name, Phone, Email.

7) Add or remove contact options, and they'll sync with FaceTime.

How to Make a FaceTime Call from Your Mac

Here's how to start a video or audio call:

1) Launch the FaceTime app and make sure you're signed in.
2) Search for your contact using their name, email, or number linked to their Apple ID.
3) Click the video camera icon for a video call, or the audio icon (or "i" for more options) for an audio-only chat.

Tip: If the person isn't signed in or their info isn't linked to FaceTime, your call won't go through.

How to Receive FaceTime Calls on a Mac

To answer a FaceTime call:

1) Make sure FaceTime is open and you're signed in.
2) When someone calls, a notification will appear on your screen.
3) Click Accept to answer or Decline to ignore.
4) Hit the red phone icon to end the call when you're done.

Don't Want to Be Disturbed?

You can temporarily disable FaceTime like this:

1) Open the app.
2) Click FaceTime > Preferences > Sign Out.
3) Need a break from specific people? Just right-click their name in FaceTime and select Block this Caller.

How to Use Email to FaceTime

No phone number? No problem. As long as the other person has FaceTime set up with an email, just type that email into the search bar and give them a call. If the email isn't linked to an Apple ID, it won't work—so double-check with them first.

How to Customize Your FaceTime Experience

Want to make the most of your screen during a call?

1) Go full screen: Click the green + icon (or hover for options) to fill your screen.
2) Change your view: Drag the picture-in-picture window showing yourself to a different corner.
3) Rotate your video: Hover over your mini window and click the rotate icon (or use gestures on a trackpad).

4) Always keep FaceTime on top: From the menu bar, choose Video > Always on Top to prevent the window from being hidden by others.

Whether you're catching up with your best friend, checking in with family, or having a quick meeting, FaceTime on a Mac is a powerful and easy way to connect. Once you get the hang of it, you'll wonder how you ever lived without it.

How to Pause or Mute a FaceTime Call

Need a quick break during a FaceTime call without ending it? You've got options!

Pause the Video:

Click the yellow minimize button at the top-left corner of the FaceTime window. This will hide the video on your screen and pause your camera feed — but don't worry, the audio keeps going, so you can still hear the other person.

To jump back in, simply click the FaceTime icon in the Dock, and you're back live on video.

Mute Yourself:

Prefer to stay on screen but silence your mic? Here's how:

Hover your mouse over the FaceTime window.

Click the Mute button when it appears.

You'll still be able to hear the other person, but they won't hear you — perfect for those unexpected background noises.

Adjusting Volume:

Want to tweak the call volume? Just use the volume keys on your Mac to turn it up or down.

How to Clear Recent FaceTime Calls

If you'd rather keep your call history private, here's how to clear it:

1) Open FaceTime.
2) To remove a specific call, right-click on it and select Remove from Recents.
3) Want a clean slate? Scroll to the bottom and click Remove all Recents.
4) That's it — your recent calls list is cleared!

How to Change Your FaceTime Ringtone

Bored with the default ringtone? Switch it up! Here's how:

1) Open FaceTime > Preferences.
2) Go to the Settings tab.

3) Click the box next to Ringtone to open the menu.
4) Choose a new ringtone from the list.
5) You can even assign custom ringtones to specific contacts:
   a) Open the Contacts app (press Command + Space, then type "Contacts").
   b) Find and select the person.
   c) Click Edit.
   d) Scroll to Ringtone, click the arrows, and pick a unique tone.

How to Take a Live Photo During a FaceTime Call

Want to capture a moment from your video call? You can take a Live Photo during the chat.

Just tap the white shutter button that appears on the screen. The person on the other end will get a quick notification that a photo was taken.

CHAPTER SEVEN

HOW TO RECORD A VIDEO ON YOUR MAC

Sure, you might instinctively reach for your phone or a fancy camera when it's time to shoot a video—but did you know your Mac can handle it, too? That's right! Whether you're creating content, hopping on a virtual meeting, or just goofing around, your Mac has everything you need to start recording right away. Let's walk through how to do it quickly and easily.

Get Your Webcam Ready

If you're using a MacBook or an iMac, you're already set—those have built-in webcams ready to go. But if you're on a Mac Mini or Mac Pro, you'll need to plug in an external webcam. Don't worry—it's typically as simple as connecting it to a USB port.

Want to go pro? You can also hook up a DSLR or mirrorless camera from brands like Canon, Sony, or Nikon with a bit of software setup. It's a great way to boost video quality if you're feeling ambitious.

How to Use Photo Booth

Every Mac comes with an app called Photo Booth. It's a simple tool that lets you snap pics or record videos using your webcam. Here's how to launch it:

1) Open Finder (the blue smiley face in your Dock), go to Applications, and double-click Photo Booth.
2) Hit Command + Spacebar to bring up Spotlight, type "Photo Booth," then press Enter.
3) Tap F4 to open Launchpad, scroll to find Photo Booth, and click it.

Switch to Video Mode

Once Photo Booth opens, you'll see yourself in the preview window, but you're not recording just yet. Look in the lower-left corner for a small video camera icon—click that to switch to video mode. Now, the red button will show a little camcorder symbol, and you're ready to roll!

Ready, Set, Record

Here's your step-by-step to make a video:

1) Open Photo Booth.
2) Click the video camera icon to switch modes.
3) Hit the big red button to start recording.
4) Hit it again to stop recording.
5) Click the thumbnail of your video in the filmstrip below to watch it back.

Right-click the thumbnail and select Export to save it wherever you like.

Tip: You can keep an eye on how long you've been recording by checking the timer in the lower-left corner. The only limit is how much free space you've got on your Mac.

Have Some Fun With Effects

Photo Booth isn't just for basic recordings—you can spice things up! Click the Effects button in the lower-right corner to explore a variety of filters and visual tricks. Use the arrows to flip through multiple pages of effects, and if you ever want to go back to normal, just choose the "Normal" option in the center.

Got More Than One Camera or Mic?

If you're using multiple webcams or external mics, no worries—you can choose which one to use. Just head to the Camera menu at the top-left of your screen (in the menu bar), and switch to the device you want.

And that's it! With just a few clicks, you can record a video right on your Mac—no extra gear required. Whether it's a quick vlog, a video message, or your next viral masterpiece, your Mac's ready when you are.

HOW TO EDIT PHOTOS AND VIDEOS IN PHOTOS FOR MAC

Whether you're just touching up vacation pics or turning your Mac into your editing studio, Photos for Mac is packed with powerful tools that make it easy to enhance your media. The best part? All edits are non-destructive, meaning you can always go back to the original image if you change your mind.

From basic brightness tweaks to advanced adjustments like selective color or vignette, here's your ultimate guide to making the most of Photos on your Mac.

How to Adjust Brightness

Want to brighten up a dull photo? Here's how:

1) Open the Photos app.
2) Double-click the photo you want to edit.
3) Click Edit in the top-right corner.
4) Drag the Light slider left or right to change the brightness.
5) Hit Done when you're happy with the result.

How to Adjust Color Saturation

Give your images a vibrant pop:

1) Launch Photos and select a photo.
2) Click Edit.
3) Use the Color slider to boost or tone down saturation.
4) Click Done to save changes.

How to Convert to Black & White

For a timeless touch:

1) Open a photo and click Edit.
2) Drag the Black & White slider to apply the effect.
3) Tweak settings like Tone, Grain, and Neutrals if desired.
4) Click Done.
5) Access Advanced Tools (Histogram, Sharpen, and More)

Go beyond the basics:

1) With a photo open in Edit mode, click the arrow next to tools like Retouch, Noise Reduction, or Vignette.
2) Adjust the sliders to fine-tune your image.
3) Click Done when finished.

Tools available:

1) Histogram: See how color and light are distributed.
2) Sharpen/Definition: Bring out detail.
3) White Balance: Fix color casts.
4) Vignette: Add dramatic edges.

How to Use Retouch for Quick Fixes

Remove blemishes or tiny distractions in seconds:

1) Open a photo and click Edit.
2) Expand the Retouch section.
3) Adjust the brush size.
4) Click or drag over areas you want to clean up.
5) Hold the Option and click to sample a texture if needed.
6) Hit Done when you're finished.

Fix Red-Eye

1) Go into Edit mode.
2) Select Red-eye from the sidebar.
3) Use the slider to adjust the brush size.
4) Click the affected eye(s).
5) Done!

Add a Filter

Want a quick artistic effect? Filters are your best friend.

1) Open a photo, and click Edit.
2) Select Filters from the top.
3) Browse and apply one that fits your vibe.
4) Click Done.

Crop, Straighten, and Rotate

Auto Crop & Straighten:

1) Click Edit → Crop.
2) Click Auto in the bottom right.
3) Done!

Manual Crop:

1) In Crop, click the arrow next to Aspect.
2) Pick a ratio or drag corners to free-crop.
3) Done!

Straighten:

1) Use the dial-in Crop to rotate and align.
2) Done!

Rotate:

1) Use the Image menu or press Command–R to rotate counterclockwise.
2) For clockwise, use Option–Command–R.

Flip:

Under the Image menu, choose Flip Horizontal or Flip Vertical.

Trim Videos

Quickly clean up the beginning or end of your videos:

1) Open a video and hover to reveal controls.
2) Click the gear icon, then select Trim.
3) Drag the yellow handles to set your trim range.
4) Click Trim to apply.

How to Reset Video Trim

Change your mind?

1) Open the video.
2) Click the gear icon.
3) Choose Reset Trim.

Want More Video Edits? Use iMovie!

Photos are great for quick trims, but for more serious video editing, bring your footage into iMovie:

Open iMovie and start a new project.

1) Select Photos Library to import your video.
2) Drag it to your timeline and edit away with transitions, text, effects, and more!

3) Export it and drag it back to Photos for safekeeping.

With just a few clicks, Photos for Mac transforms your raw shots into eye-catching images and polished videos. It's simple enough for beginners, but powerful enough to impress. So go ahead—make those memories picture-perfect.

HOW TO USE OPENAI'S NEW CHATGPT APP FOR MAC

In May 2024, OpenAI unveiled its highly anticipated ChatGPT app for Mac, finally giving desktop users a powerful native experience. While the rollout is happening in stages, ChatGPT Plus subscribers can get early access — and there's even a little-known shortcut that can get you in sooner.

Whether you're tackling a project, brainstorming ideas, or just need a quick summary of a file, the Mac app is designed to integrate seamlessly into your workflow. Here's why this app could quickly become your go-to AI assistant on macOS.

Meet the ChatGPT Launcher

Until now, Mac users have mostly relied on a browser to access ChatGPT, but the desktop app changes the game. Just tap Option + Space to summon the new ChatGPT Launcher, a compact window that floats above everything else on your screen — kind of like macOS Spotlight, but way smarter.

From there, you can immediately ask a question, start a project, or upload a file using the paperclip icon, which also unlocks some surprisingly powerful tools...

How to Take Screenshots and Query Anything

Clicking the paperclip lets you capture a screenshot of any open app or window — even ones minimized or behind others — and instantly send it to ChatGPT. Whether you're trying to summarize an article, extract content, or troubleshoot a weird setting, it can handle it.

In one test, we had ChatGPT summarize an Apple Music article, pulling insights from critic reviews. In another, it extracted and formatted text from a dropdown menu into clean HTML. It's your on-demand research assistant.

How to Use Your Camera — Or Even Your iPhone

Another neat trick: Click "Take a Photo" and your Mac's camera opens up. Just point something at the lens and ask ChatGPT about it.

Even better, you can switch to your iPhone's camera, giving you more flexibility for capturing detailed shots or items not near your Mac. The only hiccup the capture button still stays on the Mac screen something OpenAI will likely smooth out soon.

How to Customize Your ChatGPT Experience

Head to ChatGPT Settings... in the menu bar and you'll find a treasure trove of customization options. You can:

1) Control whether your content helps train the model
2) Change the Launcher shortcut
3) Enable or disable advanced features like web browsing, DALL·E, and code interpretation.

You can even set custom instructions to tailor how ChatGPT replies. Want it to be more concise, or answer like a sci-fi author or a business analyst? Just tell it how you want it to respond — it's like prompt engineering made simple.

How to Talk to ChatGPT — Literally

Inside the app's main window, you can start a voice chat or dictate your message. While there's currently a slight delay between responses and you need to wait for ChatGPT to finish speaking before replying, it's still a pretty cool feature.

OpenAI recently showcased a real-time voice mode with natural back-and-forth conversation and the ability to interrupt ChatGPT mid-sentence — and while it's not in the Mac app yet, it's coming soon with the rollout of GPT-4o.

Why the ChatGPT Mac App Is Worth Using

For anyone who uses ChatGPT regularly, the native Mac app offers a smoother, faster, and more intuitive experience. The Launcher shortcut alone makes it feel like a natural part of macOS and features like screenshot analysis, camera input, and voice interaction show where OpenAI is headed next.

With more updates on the horizon — including deeper screen understanding and real-time voice chat — this app is shaping up to be an essential productivity tool for Mac users.

CHAPTER EIGHT

HOW TO ZOOM OUT ON A MAC

Whether you're trying to see more of your screen or zoom in for a closer look, macOS gives you a ton of flexibility when it comes to zooming. From keyboard shortcuts to gesture controls, you've got multiple ways to navigate your screen like a pro.

In this guide, we'll walk you through all the different ways you can zoom out (and in!) on your Mac. Whether you prefer using your keyboard, mouse, or trackpad, you'll find a method that suits your workflow perfectly.

How to Zoom Out on Mac

Want a quick shortcut?

Just press Option + Command + Minus (–) to instantly zoom out.

It's the easiest way to get a wider view without diving into settings.

But there's more! Let's explore all the options macOS offers.

1) Open System Settings
   a) First, you'll need to make sure zoom features are enabled.
   b) Click the Apple menu □ and choose System Settings.
2) Head to Accessibility

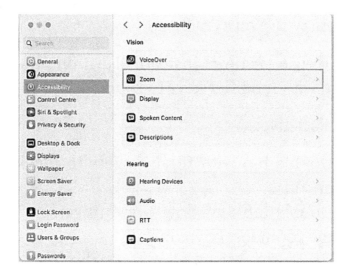

a) In the sidebar, select Accessibility, and then click Zoom under the Vision section on the right.

3) Use Keyboard Shortcuts to Zoom
   a) Toggle "Use keyboard shortcuts to zoom" to turn it on (the switch will go green).
   b) Once it's enabled, here's what you can do:
      i. Zoom In: Press Option + Command + = (equals sign)
      ii. Zoom Out: Press Option + Command + – (minus sign)
      iii. Toggle Zoom On/Off: Press Option + Command + 8

This method is super handy when you're working quickly and want instant control.

4) Zoom with Your Trackpad

Want to use gestures instead? Turn on "Use scroll gesture with modifier keys to zoom."

Once it's active:

a) Double-tap with three fingers to toggle zoom on/off
b) Double-tap and drag three fingers to control the zoom level dynamically
c) Great for MacBook users who rely on the trackpad!

5) Use Scroll to Zoom with a Mouse or Trackpad

If you prefer using a scroll wheel or two-finger swipe to zoom, here's how:

a) Enable "Use scroll gesture with modifier keys to zoom"
b) Choose your Modifier key (Control, Option, or Command)

Now, just hold the modifier key and scroll to zoom in or out. You can even change the modifier key to match your personal preference.

6) Pick Your Zoom Style

Want to customize how the zoom looks on screen? macOS gives you three display options:

a) Full Screen – Zooms the entire screen
b) Split Screen – One half of the screen shows the zoomed-in area
c) Picture-in-Picture – A small zoom window follows your pointer

For Split Screen and Picture-in-Picture, you can adjust the Size and Location to suit your needs.

7) Make Text Easier to Read

If it's just text that's too small, you don't need to zoom the whole screen.

Turn on Hover Text to display a larger version of the text under your pointer when you hold Control.

Click the little (i) icon next to it to tweak things like font size, font type, and colors for even better visibility.

Tip: Once you've explored these features, you'll find the combo that works best for you. Whether you're editing photos, reading the fine print, or simply navigating your desktop with more comfort, zooming in and out on your Mac has never been easier.

HOW TO UPDATE YOUR MACBOOK AIR

Keeping your MacBook Air up to date is essential for getting the latest features, performance improvements, and critical security patches. Whether you're rocking a newer macOS or holding onto an older version, here's how to safely update your Mac without a hitch.

Before You Begin: Back It Up!

Even though updates usually go off without a hitch, it's always wise to back up your system beforehand—just in case. The easiest way? Use Time Machine, macOS's built-in backup tool.

Here's how:

1) Connect an external hard drive (USB, Thunderbolt, or FireWire).
2) Click the Apple menu > System Preferences > Time Machine.
3) Choose Select Backup Disk, pick your drive, and check Encrypt backups if you'd like.
4) Click Use Disk to begin the backup. Time Machine will handle future backups automatically as long as it stays connected.

How to Update macOS Mojave (10.14) and Later

If your Mac is running Mojave or anything newer like Catalina, Big Sur, Monterey, or Ventura, here's how to check for updates:

1) Open the Apple menu and choose System Preferences.

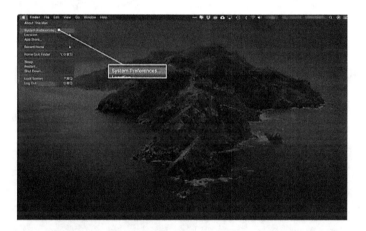

2) Select Software Update.

3) If an update is available, click Update Now to begin the process.

Tip: If you see the message "Your Mac is up to date," then you're all set!

Depending on the size of the update, the download and installation process can take anywhere from a few minutes to about an hour. Just be patient, and don't turn off your laptop during the update!

Heads-Up for Older Macs: Some users with older models have reported issues when upgrading to macOS Monterey. Double-check your Mac's compatibility on Apple's official website before taking the plunge.

How to Update macOS High Sierra (10.13) or Earlier

Still using High Sierra, El Capitan, or even Yosemite? No worries—your update route is just a little different:

1) Open the App Store on your Mac.
2) Head to the Updates tab at the top of the window.
3) If an update is listed, click Update and follow the prompts.
4) Once the update is installed, your Mac will restart automatically. Again, time varies depending on how large the update is.

Can Your Mac Handle the Latest macOS?

Not every MacBook Air can run the newest version of macOS. Here's a quick rundown to help you figure out if your machine is eligible:

1) macOS Big Sur (11): MacBook Air from 2013 or newer
2) macOS Mojave / Catalina: Mid-2012 or newer
3) macOS Sierra / High Sierra: Late 2010 or newer
4) OS X El Capitan / Yosemite: Late 2008 or newer

To find out your MacBook Air's model and current operating system:

1) Click the Apple menu and select About This Mac.
2) You'll see your macOS version and MacBook model info in the window that appears.
3) Use this information to determine which macOS version you can upgrade to.

Updating your MacBook Air doesn't have to be intimidating. With a proper backup and a few clicks, you can enjoy the latest features and keep your system running securely. Whether you're on an older version or just looking to stay current, these steps have you covered!

HOW TO BACK UP AND RESTORE YOUR MAC USING TIME MACHINE

Let's face it—tech fails sometimes. That's why backing up your Mac regularly is essential. The good news macOS has your back with a built-in tool called Time Machine. It's powerful and straightforward, and once it's set up, it practically runs itself.

How to Back Up Your Mac With Time Machine

Time Machine is macOS's free backup solution that automatically keeps your files safe. It stores:

1) Hourly backups for the past 24 hours
2) Daily backups for the past month
3) Weekly backups for everything older—until your backup drive fills up
4) And if you're on the go? It even saves local snapshots to your internal storage for quick access when your backup drive isn't handy.

How to Set It Up

1) Pick a backup drive. This can be an external hard drive or SSD.
2) Plug it into your Mac. You might see a prompt— click "Allow".
3) Head to System Settings > General > Time Machine, then click "Add Backup Disk".
4) Choose your drive and hit "Set Up Disk."

You can also enable encryption for security and limit how much space the backups take up (handy for larger drives). Note: Setting up Time Machine will erase the drive, so back up anything important before starting.

After that, Time Machine will begin the initial backup. It might take a while but this one captures everything. Afterward, only new and changed files will be backed up, so things move much faster.

How to Customize What Gets Backed Up

Don't want to back up everything? No problem. Click "Options" in the Time Machine settings to exclude folders like your Applications folder or other large directories you don't need copies of.

How to Back Up to Multiple Drives

Want extra peace of mind? Add more backup disks. Time Machine will rotate between them, giving you multiple copies across different locations.

Local Snapshots

Even when you're not connected to your backup drive, Time Machine still has your back. It keeps daily and weekly snapshots right on your Mac's internal storage. That means you can still recover deleted files or older versions even on the go.

Automatic vs. Manual Backups

By default, Time Machine runs automatically every hour when the backup drive is connected. You can unplug it during the day and plug it back in later—Time Machine will pick up right where it left off.

Prefer more control? Switch to manual backups:

1) In Time Machine settings, go to "Options" and set the backup frequency to Manual.
2) Then, use the Time Machine menu bar icon and click "Back Up Now" whenever you want.
3) You can also set automatic backups to run daily or weekly instead of hourly if that suits your workflow better.

How to Restore Individual Files

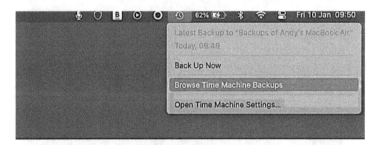

Need to retrieve a deleted file or an older version? Here's how:

1) Click the Time Machine icon in the menu bar and choose "Browse Time Machine Backups."

2) Navigate through a Finder-style interface. Use the timeline on the right to scroll through different backup dates.
3) Red dates = stored on your external backup drive
4) White dates = local snapshots on your Mac
5) Find your file using the search bar or manually browse.
6) Select it and hit "Restore."

Time Machine will place it right back where it originally lived. If there's a conflict, you'll get the option to keep both or replace the existing file.

How to Restore an Entire Mac

Time Machine can restore your entire Mac to a previous state—perfect if you're recovering from a major crash or setting up a new machine.

To do this:

1) Shut down your Mac and then hold the power button until you see "Loading Startup Options."
2) Choose "Options" to boot into macOS Recovery Mode.
3) Select "Restore from Time Machine Backup" and follow the on-screen steps.
4) On older Intel Macs, just hold Command + R when booting up to get into Recovery Mode.

How to Move Time Machine Backups to a New Mac

Got a new Mac? You can bring all your files over using Migration Assistant:

1) Open Applications > Utilities > Migration Assistant (or search for it with Spotlight).
2) Plug in your Time Machine drive.
3) Follow the prompts to import your apps, settings, and files from the backup.
4) This also works during initial setup—plug in your backup, and macOS will ask if you want to restore from it.

How to Access Time Machine Backups on Windows

Time Machine is made for Macs—but if you need to access your backup from a Windows PC, you'll need a little help.

macOS uses the APFS file system, which Windows doesn't support. To open the drive, you'll need a third-party tool like:

1) Paragon APFS for Windows
2) TransMac

These apps aren't free, but free trials are usually enough for quick access. Keep in mind:

1) If your Time Machine backup is encrypted, Windows won't be able to read it.
2) You won't get a fancy interface—just a file tree to browse and copy what you need.
3) If you're switching completely to Windows, it's better to reformat the drive once you've recovered your files.
4) Time Machine is one of the easiest backup tools out there. Once it's set up, it runs quietly in the background, making sure you never lose your files—even if your Mac takes a dive or you delete something by mistake.

CHAPTER NINE

HOW TO WIPE A MACBOOK AIR

Whether you're preparing to sell your MacBook Air, gift it to someone, or simply want a fresh start, wiping your MacBook and resetting it to factory settings are a great way to go. This guide will walk you through the process of erasing all data, ensuring your device is ready for its next user—or a brand-new macOS installation.

The steps outlined here are for macOS Big Sur (11.0) and later, though earlier macOS versions follow similar procedures.

How to Back Up Your Data

Before you erase anything, it's critical to back up your data to ensure you don't lose anything important. Use Time Machine to back up to an external storage device.

1) Plug in your external storage device to your MacBook.
2) Open System Preferences and select Time Machine.
3) Click Select Disk and choose your external drive.
4) Select Use Disk, and the backup will start. The initial backup may take several hours depending on how much data is stored on your device.
5) Time Machine is reliable and will ensure you can restore your files later.

Sign Out of iCloud and Other Services.

Before wiping your Mac, sign out of iCloud and services like Find My Mac to prevent the next user from being asked for your credentials. Here's how:

1) Open System Preferences, and then select Apple ID (or iCloud in older versions).
2) Click Sign Out. You might be asked for your password to confirm.
3) When prompted, choose to keep a copy of your iCloud data if you wish.

Wipe Your MacBook Air and Reinstall macOS.

Now it's time to erase everything. Follow these steps to wipe your Mac and reinstall macOS, leaving it in like-new condition:

1) Shut down your MacBook Air.
2) Hold down the Command + R keys and press the power button to start up in Recovery Mode.
3) Once the Apple logo or spinning globe appears, release the keys.
4) In macOS Utilities, select Reinstall macOS and click Continue.
5) You may be asked to unlock your disk or enter your password before proceeding.

Let the MacBook restart and reinstall macOS. The process will take some time, with several restarts and a progress bar to show the installation status.

Once completed, your Mac will boot to the Setup Assistant. If you're selling or gifting it, press Command+Q to quit the setup process and shut down the computer. Now it's ready for its next owner.

How to Erase Your MacBook Without Reinstalling macOS

If you just want to completely clear your device without reinstalling the operating system, you can follow these steps:

1) Shut down your MacBook Air.
2) Press Command + R and turn on the MacBook while holding down the keys to boot into Recovery Mode.
3) Once in the macOS Utilities window, choose Disk Utility.
4) Under the View menu, select Show All Devices.
5) Select your primary drive (usually named Macintosh HD), and then click Erase.
6) Confirm the action and hit Erase again to wipe everything from the disk.

Once the process is complete, your MacBook will display a flashing question mark in a folder icon, indicating no operating system is installed.

How to Choose Your macOS Installation Version

When booting into Recovery Mode, you can choose different versions of macOS to install:

1) Press Option + Command + R to install the latest macOS that's compatible with your MacBook.
2) Press Shift + Option + Command + R to install the macOS version that originally came with your MacBook.

How to Use the New "Erase All Content and Settings" Feature (macOS Monterey and Later)

If you're running macOS Monterey (12.0) or newer, Apple introduced an easier and faster way to erase your Mac without reinstalling the operating system. This feature, similar to the one found on iPhones, wipes all your data and apps but leaves macOS intact. Here's how to use it:

1) Open System Preferences.
2) Select Erase All Content and Settings from the System Preferences menu.

3) Follow the prompts to complete the process.
4) This method is quicker than a full system reinstall and ensures all your data is wiped.

HOW TO FIND APPS ON YOUR MACBOOK

Just switched from a Windows PC to a MacBook? You might be wondering where all your apps went! Unlike Windows, macOS does things a little differently—there's no Start menu or cluttered desktop filled with shortcuts. But don't worry, macOS gives you a few easy and powerful ways to find and launch your apps. Let's walk through the top four methods to track down your apps in no time.

1) Applications Folder

Think of the Applications folder as your central app library. It holds everything—from built-in Apple apps to anything you've installed from the App Store.

Here's how to get there:

a) Click the Finder icon on your Dock (it's the smiley face).

b) In the Finder window, select Applications from the left sidebar.

c) Once you're inside, you'll see a full list of your apps. Double-click to launch any app, or right-click for options like:

Get Info – See how much space the app is using.

Move to Bin – Uninstall apps you no longer need.

Add to Dock – Just drag the app to your Dock for quicker access in the future.

2) Launchpad: Like an iPad Home Screen for Mac

Launchpad is Apple's way of making app browsing feel more familiar to iPhone and iPad users. It displays your apps in a grid layout—just like your mobile device.

To open Launchpad:

a) Click the Launchpad icon (the one with nine little squares) in your Dock.
b) Now you'll see all your apps. You can:
c) Double-click any app to launch it.
d) Use the search bar at the top if you have too many to scroll through.
e) Create folders by dragging one app onto another—just like on iOS.

3) Spotlight Search: Fast and Efficient

When you know exactly what you're looking for, Spotlight Search is your best friend. It's super quick and doesn't require digging through folders or menus.

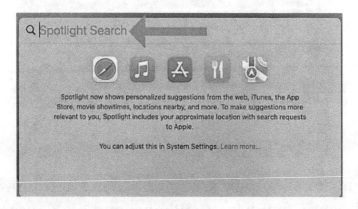

To bring it up, you can either:

a) Press Command + Space, or
b) Tap the F4 key (on some Macs).
c) Just start typing the name of the app you want—like "Spotify" or "Photos"—and it'll show up instantly in the results. Click to open. Easy!

4) Ask Siri: Open Apps With Your Voice

Why click when you can just talk? Siri is built right into macOS and can help you open apps in seconds—no hands required.

To activate Siri:

a) Click the Siri icon in the menu bar or Dock,
b) Or say "Hey Siri" if you've enabled voice activation.
c) Then just say something like:
d) "Open Safari" or "Launch Notes", and Siri takes care of the rest.

Tip: Once you find a favorite app, drag it to your Dock for one-click access at any time.

With these four handy methods—Applications Folder, Launchpad, Spotlight Search, and Siri—you'll never waste time hunting down an app again. Whether you're a visual browser, a keyboard ninja, or a voice-command enthusiast, macOS has a solution tailored just for you.

HOW TO OPEN, CLOSE, MINIMIZE & ZOOM ON YOUR MACBOOK AIR

Windows on a Mac aren't just pieces of glass—they're the digital frames where your apps live and breathe. Each one shows you a slice of whatever program you're running, whether it's Safari, Pages, or your favorite music app. Some apps stick to one window, others multiply like rabbits (we're looking at you, Finder!).

How to Open and Close Windows

When you click on an app's icon in the Dock or Applications folder, it usually opens a window—or jumps to one that's already open. Want more than one window? Here's how:

1) Go to File > New Window (or something similar to New Document).
2) Hit Command + N on your keyboard.
3) Command-click the app icon in the Dock and select New Window (works in some apps).

Need to close a window? Easy:

1) Click the red button in the top-left corner of the window.
2) Or choose File > Close Window.
3) Or just tap Command + W.
4) To close all open windows in an app: File > Close All Windows.

Tip: Closing a window doesn't always quit the app. You'll still see a small dot under its Dock icon, showing it's still running. To shut it down completely, go to the app name in the Menu bar and click Quit or press Command + Q.

How to Minimize Windows

Do too many windows cluttering your screen? Minimize the ones you're not using—but still want close by:

1) Click the yellow minimize button (top-left corner of the window).
2) Use the Window > Minimize menu option.
3) Or tap Command + M.
4) Want to minimize all windows of an app at once? Press Command + Option + M.

To bring a window back:

1) Click its icon in the Dock.
2) Command-click the Dock icon and select Open.
3) Go to the Window menu of the app and select it from the list.
4) Choose Window > Bring All to Front to bring all that app's windows forward.
5) Hold Option and go to Window > Arrange in Front to neatly cascade windows.

6) In Safari, you can even hit Window > Merge All Windows to pull all your minimized ones into tab view.

Maximizing and Zooming Windows: What's the Deal?

Here's where Mac and Windows part ways. On a Mac, you don't maximize a window—you zoom it. But there's also Full Screen, and the difference matters.

To go Full Screen:

1) Click the green button in the top-left corner.
2) Click it again or use View > Exit Full Screen (or press Control + Command + F) to exit.
3) Zoom, on the other hand, is for those who want the window to resize to its "best fit" without necessarily filling the entire screen. Here's how to zoom in:
4) Hold the Option and click the green button.
5) Or choose Window > Zoom from the menu.

Need more control? Drag any of the window's corners to size it exactly how you want. When you're done tinkering, you can always hit Window > Zoom to snap it back to optimal size.

Master these shortcuts and controls, and you'll never feel overwhelmed by windows again—unless it's the weather.

HOW TO CHANGE YOUR MAC LOGIN PICTURE

To update your profile photo, head to System Preferences > Users & Groups > Edit, choose an image, then hit Save.

To change your Mac's login wallpaper, go to System Preferences > Desktop & Screen Saver and pick a new background.

Changing your login photo also updates it across all devices linked to your Apple ID.

How to Give Your Mac a Personal Touch

Whether you're tired of the default icon or just feel like freshening things up, changing your Mac's login picture is easy—and kind of fun. Here's a step-by-step guide to get you started.

How to Change Your Mac Login Picture

1) Click the Apple menu in the top-left corner of your screen.

2) Go to System Preferences, then select Users & Groups.
3) Click your current profile picture. A new window will pop up with several options.
4) Now comes the fun part. You can choose from:
    a) Memoji: Create or select a custom animated character.
    b) Emoji: Keep it light with a classic emoji.
    c) Monogram: A clean, stylish take on your initials.
    d) Camera: Snap a new photo with your Mac's built-in camera.
    e) Photos: Choose from your photo library.
    f) Suggestions: Browse Apple's curated images.

Once you've chosen an image, it will preview in the corner. For certain images like Memoji, you can fine-tune the look by:

a) Zooming in/out using a slider.
b) Dragging the image within the frame.
c) Selecting a pose or background color.

When you're happy with how it looks, click Save. That's it—your updated login image will now appear next to your name on the login screen.

This image is tied to your Apple ID, so it'll also show up on any other Apple devices signed in with the same account.

How to Change Your Mac's Login Screen Wallpaper

Your login screen background is simply a reflection of your desktop wallpaper. So if you want a new vibe every time you boot up your Mac, here's what to do:

1) Open the Apple menu and choose System Preferences.
2) Select Wallpaper (or Desktop & Screen Saver on older macOS versions).
3) Browse and pick from Apple's categories like:
4) Dynamic Wallpapers (change with the time of day)
5) Landscapes, Cityscapes, Underwater, Earth, Aerials, and more
6) Solid Colors for a minimal aesthetic

Or, head to Pictures to use images from your photo library

Want to use your collection?

Click the Add Photo Add Folder or Album dropdowns, and then select Choose Folder to add your image folder.

Tip: Make sure the image matches your screen resolution—otherwise, it might look stretched or blurry.

By tweaking your login photo and background, you're giving your Mac a little more personality—and making your experience that much more enjoyable every time you log in.

INDEX

www.ingramcontent.com/pod-product-compliance
Lightning Source LLC
LaVergne TN
LVHW051341050326
832903LV00031B/3680